THE ENNEAGRAM PERSONALITY PORTRAITS

Improving Problem-Solving Skills
Participant Workbook

Patrick J. Aspell, Ph.D.
Dee Dee Aspell, M.A.

ISBN: 0-7879-0886-X

Published by

An Imprint of Jossey-Bass Inc., Publishers
350 Sansome Street, Fifth Floor
San Francisco, California 94104-1342
(415) 433-1740; Fax (415) 433-0499
(800) 274-4434; Fax (800) 569-0443

Pfeiffer

Visit our website at: http://www.pfeiffer.com

Outside of the United States, Pfeiffer products can be purchased from the following Simon & Schuster International Offices:

Prentice Hall Canada
PTR Division
1870 Birchmont Road
Scarborough, Ontario M1P2J7
Canada
(800) 567-3800; Fax (800) 263-7733

Prentice Hall
Campus 400
Maylands Avenue
Hemel Hempstead
Hertfordshire HP2 7EZ
United Kingdom
44(0) 1442 881891; Fax 44(0) 1442 882288

Prentice Hall Professional
Locked Bag 531
Frenchs Forest PO NSW 2068
Australia
61 2 9907 5693; Fax 61 2 0095 7934

Prentice Hall/Pfeiffer
P.O. Box 1636
Randburg 2125
South Africa
27 11 781 0780; Fax 27 11 781 0781

Simon & Schuster (Asia) Pte Ltd.
317 Alexandra Road
#04-01 IKEA Building
Singapore 159965
Asia
65 476 4688; Fax 65 378 0370

ACKNOWLEDGMENTS

It is said that if we see farther than our ancestors, it is because we stand on the shoulders of those who preceded us. We too are indebted to the teachers and writers who have mined and discovered the hidden riches of the Enneagram: Gurdjieff, Ichazo, Naranjo, Beesing, Condon, Dobson and Hurley, Palmer, Riso, Rohr, and Wagner. All made original contributions to the development of the Enneagram.

Although we have milked many cows, the butter is our own. We have applied the Enneagram in many unique ways to business and organizations, as well as to education, psychology, and religion. Fortunately, we have been supported on our Enneagram journey by many friends. Our many thanks go out to the following:

- Marian Prokop, who was the prime mover of this Enneagram project and is the expert editor of our works;

- Maryann Morabito, who was an invaluable computer supporter;

- Jack Labanauskas and Andrea Isaacs, co-editors of the *Enneagram Monthly*, who published our many articles on the applications of the Enneagram to business, education, and counseling;

- Maurice and Tolina Doublet, Dee Dee's parents, who have encouraged us through the long years of Enneagram writing;

- David and Juanita Hammeren, our first printers, who believed in us and trusted in our dream;

- All the subjects who graciously consented to take The Enneagram Inventory® from its first version through its many drafts;

- Patrick, our son, whose patience and understanding allows us to devote long hours of labor to give birth to these materials; and

- God, who shared infinite gifts with us and brought our work to fruition.

CONTENTS

1

INTRODUCTION

Welcome to the Enneagram way of thinking and problem solving! Through the activities in this workbook, you will learn insights and ideas to help you develop knowledge and skills in thinking and problem solving, such as the following:

∎ Understanding of the nine personality types and three centers of personalities;

∎ Strengths and limitations of the nine styles of thinking;

∎ Behavioral hints to recognize the nine thinking styles;

∎ The nine focuses that give direction and purpose to thinking;

∎ Ways to transform thinking style by using the "arrows" and "wings" of development;

∎ Five ways to improve each thinking style;

∎ Cues to access the appropriate thinking style; and

∎ Nine approaches to problem solving.

To accomplish these objectives, the chapters build on one another, as follows:

∎ The person who is thinking. What is your personality type?

∎ Thinking style. How do you think?

∎ Identification of thinking style. How do you recognize thinking styles?

∎ The focus of thinking. What are you thinking?

∎ Transformation of thinking style. How do you develop your thinking style?

∎ Strategic problem solving. How do diverse thinking styles approach problems?

Note that this workbook begins with a review of the nine Enneagram types; if you have not had the opportunity to determine your Enneagram type with *The Enneagram Personality Portraits Inventory and Profile*®, use the descriptions in Chapter 2 to decide which type is most like you. Remember that the descriptions are based on how a person of that type typically feels or behaves. You may find that you identify with more than one type; in that case, consider the one or two types that describe you best when you complete the activities that follow.

2

PERSONALITY TYPE

Team planning and development requires knowledge. Knowledge of who you are—how you think, what motivates you, how you relate to others, and your work style—empowers you to plan your team and develop your interpersonal style. Knowledge of other team members empowers you with an appreciation of their individual frames of reference. Personalities can be understood in groups of three according to their centers, as shown in Figure 1.

Gut personalities (EIGHTS, NINES, ONES) tend to be concerned about their needs in a team, i.e., who they are and how they can take care of themselves. Heart personalities (TWOS, THREES, FOURS) wonder how they are doing with others and whether or not they are meeting others' needs. Head personalities (FIVES, SIXES, SEVENS) focus on figuring out what is going on in the team.

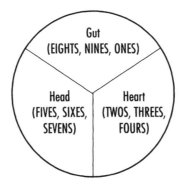

Figure 1. Three Centers of Personalities

Descriptions of Enneagram Personality Types

ONES

Perfecters like to excel in doing things well because they have high ideals. Uncomfortable with being criticized, they like to see themselves as good and right. Their strengths usually lie in the desire to be correct, conscientious, fair, and honest. However, they can be limited by the tendency to be critical, judgmental, and rigid. Their idealistic thinking is guided by objective standards and based on principles. They are motivated by the need to be right and to avoid criticism. In relationships, ONES are attracted to people who lead good lives and who value integrity and objectivity. They like to help others to improve themselves. Intimacy develops when ONES respond more to their feelings and needs than to "shoulds." They express affection in established ways at appropriate times and places. At work, ONES are generally task oriented, methodical, and hard working. Their personalities unfold as they strive for excellence and correctness. A ONE's sense of justice needs to be tempered by compassion.

TWOS

Carers are motivated by love to help others. They like to see themselves as giving and supportive. As good listeners, they tend to be empathic, friendly, and warm. However, because they are apt to be unaware of their own needs, they may find it difficult to say "no." Their affective thinking reasons from the heart or from their feelings and focuses on the concerns of others. TWOS are motivated by a need to care for and help others without being concerned about their own need to be nurtured. In relationships, TWOS are drawn to those in need, and they help in order to gain acceptance and affection. They can tend to flatter others for approval. Intimacy develops when TWOS let their own genuine needs be met by others. They are strongly committed to relationships in which they feel wanted. TWOS tend to be people oriented, altruistic, and generous in serving others. Their personalities unfold as they unselfishly fulfill the real needs of others. Their caring needs to be genuine in order to receive authentic love from others.

THREES

Achievers are motivated to succeed in reaching their goals efficiently. They like to think of themselves as worthwhile and desirable. Energetic and sociable, they are competitive and driven to attain results. Obsessed with social status, they may sacrifice relationships for career. Their enthusiasm and abilities to communicate make them effective in public relations. Their practical thinking puts ideas into action by calculating the means used for achieving results. They are motivated by a need to succeed and avoid failure. They are attracted to people with prestige and to relationships in which they can perform effectively. Assertive with people, THREES like to be close to others when they are doing something or engaged in social activities. Their personalities unfold as they are productive while being loyal to others. They need to balance success with integrity.

FOURS

Creators value introspection and sensitive awareness of their feelings and impulses. They see themselves as empathic and understanding. Desiring to be unique and genuine, they like to express their feelings creatively in both serious and humorous ways. The depth of their emotional experience enables FOURS to appreciate art. They intuit others' feelings as they listen to them at work or at home. Their individualist thinking reasons according to what is meaningful to people and their feelings. In relationships, FOURS are drawn to people who appreciate them and withdraw in the face of misunderstanding. Intimacy develops as FOURS let go of past hurts and find the good in other people. Their personalities unfold as they become aware of their unique personal goodness. Their sensitive feelings need to be balanced by rational thinking.

FIVES

Observers are attentive to data; they grasp and reflect on ideas and explain situations in the light of theories. They think of themselves as knowledgeable and insightful. Their strengths lie in logical and objective reasoning, uncontrolled by emotions. Tending to be out of contact with their feelings, FIVES are not apt to become fully involved in the social world or to take action on their ideas. Their analytical thinking observes situations, reasons logically, and explains clearly. They are motivated by the desire to know as much as they can and to avoid ignorance. Because FIVES tend to be emotionally detached in relationships, they are more comfortable sharing abstract ideas and thoughts than personal feelings. In their work, they make good facilitators because they can summarize discussions and explain logically what is happening in groups. Their detached theoretical stance enables them to plan long-range projects. Their personalities emerge as they acknowledge the limitations of their own knowledge in the face of the wonders of the universe. Their thinking needs to be balanced by feeling.

SIXES

Groupists like to relate to people within a partnership, family, team, or community. Secure in their bonds with others, they are cooperative, loyal, and reliable. They think of themselves as dependable and faithful. They respect honor, tradition, duty, and obedience to the groups to which they belong. Their thinking is based on some form of authority, such as the leader, the group, tradition, or rules. They are motivated by the need to belong to a relationship and avoid disapproval and insecurity. Insecure feelings may lead to their being indecisive and over-relying on authority. Once they are committed to a relationship, SIXES are faithful and give of themselves. However, they may find it difficult to receive from others. In their work, they are dedicated to a task or mission and collaborate with others. Their personalities are actualized as they face their fears and develop inner authority. Their fidelity needs to be directed more to the spirit of the law than to the letter of the law.

SEVENS

Cheerers are outgoing and spontaneous. Usually gifted with different skills and a variety of interests, they are enthusiastic in their enjoyment of life. They are optimistic as they look to the promising possibilities of the future. With a positive self-image, they are inclined to see themselves as happy. Usually on the go and fearful of pain, they may not appreciate the value of discomfort or suffering as challenges and opportunities for personal growth. Their positive thinking considers new and different possibilities and plans for future enjoyment. SEVENS are motivated by the need to be happy and avoid unpleasant experiences. In relationships, they are attracted to people who enjoy life. By focusing on the pleasing features of relationships, they manage problems and feel comfortable being close to other people. Ready to see the bright side of situations, they create a positive atmosphere for people to feel good at work. Their personalities emerge as they manage their impulses and deepen their appreciation of the meaning of suffering. Their anticipation of the future needs to be balanced by an appreciation of the present.

EIGHTS

Challengers are confident and easily assert themselves in deciding and taking action. They like to think of themselves as strong and powerful. They are fearless in grappling with problems and mobilizing people to get the job done. EIGHTS tend to regard gentleness as a weakness. Their type of thinking dictates opposing opinions and putting forth ideas forcefully. They are motivated by the need to be self-determining and to avoid submitting to others. Usually the dominant people in relationships, they feel capable being in charge. Intimacy develops when they are willing to be vulnerable in sharing their inner feelings. At work, EIGHTS make natural leaders and welcome difficult tasks, especially those that pertain to justice. Their personalities unfold as they come in contact with the tender side of their natures. They need to balance their caring for strength with the strength of caring.

NINES

Accepters are easy-going and stable. They get along with most people they meet. They see themselves as calm and accepting. Their patience, gentleness, and simplicity make other people feel comfortable and at ease with them. Their holistic thinking grasps similarities and plays down differences to unify different ideas into a harmonious whole. They are motivated by the need to live in unity and peace among conflicting parties. As NINES identify with people in relationships, they tend to feel close to them. Low in energy, they are not apt to control others. Their gifts of mediation enable them to harmonize differences within groups and make peace among conflicting parties. However, they may tend to gloss over problems and play down disagreements in order to avoid conflict. Their personalities are enhanced as they become more energized and enthused about developing their potential and confronting life's problems directly. Their desire for peace needs to be balanced by courage in facing the hard reality of conflicts.

Personal Reflections

Does the description of your personality type(s) fit you and how you usually experience yourself? Are the descriptive traits consistent with your personal experience of yourself? It is your decision to accept what fits how you see yourself. You can choose to reject whatever is inconsistent with your self-perception.

You may want to check the accuracy of your self-perception with the observations of someone in the team who knows you. You could invite that person to share his or her perceptions of you with you in an honest and gentle fashion. This person's agreement or disagreement with your self-perceptions can help you to discover your actual personality type. Self-discovery is a gradual, continual process of learning about yourself.

What do you think and feel about the type(s) that your reading of the descriptions of types or your responses to *The Enneagram Personality Portraits Inventory and Profile*® showed you to be?

How comfortable or uncomfortable do you feel with what your profile reflects?

What is meaningful to you about your type?

What are the strengths of your type?

How could you use your knowledge of your type to benefit you and the team?

If you are not comfortable about your type, remember to keep in mind that no type is good or bad. Simply different types of people have different interests, talents, and styles of relating. Such different talents make each type unique.

In retrospect, remember that you are exploring preferences, meaning what you usually or actually like to do. Are you currently in a leadership or team position that does not fit your usual preferences? Or are you making changes? If you answered "yes" to either of these questions, you may be experiencing discomfort between what you actually like to do and what you are doing at present.

You may want to examine the desirability of your present situation in the team. Do you need to adjust to the situation in which you find yourself, or do you need to reassess your preferences?

NOTES

3

NINE THINKING STYLES

Thinking empowers people to handle reality and deal with problems. However, different personality types think in different ways. For example, practical pragmatic thinking may work in getting a project done quickly but not be effective in coping with the feelings of disgruntled employees. The following sections describe the ways of thinking of each of the nine Enneagram types.

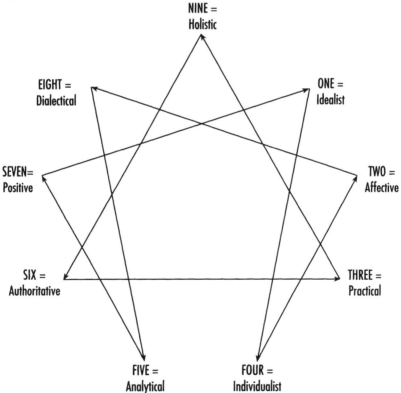

Figure 2. Nine Thinking Styles

ONES: IDEALIST THINKERS

The Idealist thinking of ONES is motivated by high personal standards and values: They think about the degree to which people and organizations measure up to ideals. ONES can be looked to for assurances that the proposed plans contain quality standards, and quality of effort is a main concern. In addition, they are concerned about ways to improve the tasks assigned to them.

ONES like goals that draw people with different viewpoints into agreement. Ambitious goals attract them, and they want to be sure their ideas conform to these goals. Points of view that contradict these ideal goals are bound to be questioned.

The minds of ONES strive to understand things accurately and thoroughly before advancing. Therefore, expert or competent opinions are respected. Because of their conscientious concern for details, ONES keep others in the organization aware of limits, such as budget and time constraints. Their proposed solutions are carefully thought out and well-formulated. They reason by taking one step at a time, appropriating new information in manageable bits.

The ideal world of ONES includes one best method for doing things. In this world, problems can be solved and the right decisions made by following proven methods and sound procedures. ONES function well in situations that require precision. Because they are uncomfortable with open-ended approaches, their strategic thinking focuses on specific aspects of an issue. Their thinking proceeds slowly but surely and correctly. They conscientiously learn the skills and thinking required to be competent at whatever they are doing.

Situations are seen in terms of good or bad, and ONES challenge themselves and others to live in moral, upright ways. They emphasize values, whether or not these values can be measured or calculated. In their concern about the way things should be, ONES tend toward prescriptive thinking. They base their conclusions on principles; because they are so sure about what should be done, ONES may come across with strong views.

In terms of limitations, anger may prevent ONES from focusing on facts. They may over-emphasize values so much that they become blinded to the facts. Rigidly applied formulas may screen out important data, and ONES may project unrealistically high goals.

Twos: Affective Thinkers

The Affective thinking of TWOS focuses on what is helpful to others and figures out ways to express warmth and friendliness. For TWOS, the heart has reasons the mind does not know. They are usually more comfortable figuring out how they are going to relate to people rather than calculating how to accomplish tasks.

Affective thinkers consider whatever is of value or importance to people—themselves as well as others. Personal values are given more weight than performance requirements. Valuing tactfulness with people over the tactics of getting a job done, affective thinkers tend to have highly developed interpersonal skills. For TWOS, appreciation has more personal meaning than accomplishment.

When TWOS feel personally supported, their minds are receptive to learning whatever is presented as they explore new things. Their natural sociability enables them to adjust to learning in new situations. Once rapport is established with members of a team or organization, they are more willing to take risks in thinking about challenging projects.

TWOS are apt to think of solutions that meet the needs of everyone concerned, and they usually have a good sense of what others need. However, they may be so preoccupied with how they are relating that they may not be clear about what they are thinking.

The Affective thinking of TWOS is apt to be more influenced by people who are closer, such as friends, than by people who are more distant, however more knowledgeable or efficient. They usually believe they understand people well and encourage them to express their views and articulate goals.

The limitations for TWOS also come as a result of their concern for others: Their feelings may easily sway them and lead to inconsistent statements. "Hard facts" may be treated lightly in order to plan broad programs that meet everyone's needs, potentially obscuring useful strategies for getting things done.

PRACTICAL
THINKERS

THREES: PRACTICAL THINKERS

The Practical thinking of THREES is motivated to achieve. THREES concentrate on the results they want to produce and calculate the means most useful to their objectives, keeping their attention and energies focused on the reachable goal. They are likely to make sure that a group is progressing toward its goals.

For THREES, their ideas are tools for putting a plan into action, even without a great deal of knowledge at the beginning. They communicate these ideas through persuasion, using words effectively to serve their interests.

THREES tend to try "whatever works" in a problem-solving situation. This approach usually means taking one step at a time, as long each is successful. Unattached to set theories, they are free to try new strategies, and any experimentation that has a good chance of producing results is likely to be tried. Forming concepts takes second place to the generating tactical approaches, and success is assessed in relation to goals. That is, the test of success is not whether a strategy is correct but whether it works.

THREES look at facts and values in terms of their usefulness in getting results. They have a knack for figuring out what people will accept, and an immediate grasp of what others want as opposed to what they need. Their efficient minds get projects done quickly, often finding shortcuts to quicken the pace. They work quickly and prefer challenging situations in which the goals are clear. They assess problems as they go along and as they experience outcomes. This adaptable approach works especially well in changing situations with many variables. Making adjustments as they go along, THREES move in one direction if it works and avoid useless steps.

This type of thinking works best when the demand is immediate progress, experimentation, innovation, and adaptability. The limitations come when, in their hurry for results, THREES treat details lightly. This kind of shortcut thinking may produce something less than quality results. Long-range planning may be screened out for short-term, immediate payoffs. Practical thinkers tend to focus on managing problems rather than solving them. As a result, high standards and consistent commitment may be forfeited for fast rewards.

FOURS: INDIVIDUALIST THINKERS

The Individualist thinking of FOURS is easily influenced by feelings. FOURS personalize their thinking; that is, they judge the value of something or some person to the extent of its importance to them personally.

"Important" to FOURS depends on acceptance or rejection by others. Their thinking is easily influenced by what they like and find pleasant about people, as well as what they dislike and experience as unpleasant. As they adapt to different situations, Individualist thinkers easily alternate between love and hate, joy and sadness, or peace and anger.

FOURS want to think in ways that are special and individual, as opposed to being absorbed into a collective or group mind. Their creative or imaginative thinking assures them of standing out from the ordinary ideas or conventional knowledge.

The empathic thinking of FOURS intuits what other people are experiencing. In addition, their tendency to share others' feelings is expressed in a sympathetic knowing that empowers them to listen attentively to the experience of others.

For Individualist thinkers, emotional state-of-mind affects how they think about things. FOURS dwell on their internal experience—inner thoughts, feelings, and images; their attention is drawn outward when they experience work or material that is appealing.

FOURS tend to think in terms of metaphors and symbols to grasp the deeper meaning of a situation. It is important for them to understand the reasons underlying the issues at hand. Their thinking is clear when they experience rapport with people, but attention to the tasks at hand may be difficult when they are tested or expected to perform.

However, FOURS may come up with utopian solutions to problems, solutions whose costs are unrealistic. Because they are so aware of feelings, they may seem overly sentimental to others. What is true in a given situation for a FOUR depends on and varies according to mood. They are apt to reason more from feelings than from facts and may allow their feelings to blind them to effective strategies.

FIVES: ANALYTICAL THINKERS

The Analytical thinking of FIVES drives them to know as much as they can. They gather and order data, measure whatever they can, figure out problems, reason logically, and look for the good method to come to a solution. They look for connections between ideas to fit them into a grand theory. It is important for their ideas to be theoretically consistent. The world in which they work is viewed as basically "rational." They usually reason from a general theory or formula to specific situations. Facts are apt to be fitted into broad rational explanations or models. General principles, such as "A penny saved is a penny earned," are self-evident to them.

FIVES can be consulted for an analysis of projects to be sure they contribute to long-range goals. Their long-term, systematic approach works well in stable situations. The attention to strategy, information, and structure can empower a team to systematically implement decisions. It is important for them to discover the meaning of facts and be certain of a solution.

Within an adequate theory, they intelligently and consistently fit different viewpoints. They want their theories to be backed by data and to predict how something can be directed toward a concrete goal. Reality for FIVES is what is logical and measurable. They are more interested in what a thing is—its essential qualities—than what it does. Their thinking is helpful in getting groups to go beyond surface issues and data. Thus, their thinking tends to be speculative and abstract. Detached from their feelings, their thinking is unlikely to be controlled by emotions.

If FIVES speculate constantly, they may resist getting down to earth with its concrete situations. When their rationally formulated theories seem real, they may behave as if their interpretations are facts. As a result, strategies may not be checked out with relevant information. If anxiety clouds their thinking, FIVES may ignore facts and impose their own ideas and theories to solve a problem. Excessive analysis may impede making timely decisions.

SIXES: AUTHORITATIVE THINKERS

The Authoritative thinking of SIXES is based on some form of authority: a leader, tradition, custom, or regulation. These forms of authority usually represent what the majority or group thinks. Their thinking can also be described as relational, because they base their conclusions more on the team than on any one individual. Consensus is important to confirm the correctness of a decision.

The assent of the team is important for decision making. SIXES are concerned about each member of a group being heard and his or her views being used for the good of the team. They are more interested in relationships than opinions.

Ideas are compared to understand situations. They are more interested in knowing the basic meaning of a problem than its surface issues. They want their ideas to be clear so they can be understood by others. Once they feel at home with the subject matter and comfortable with people, they set their mind to grasping content.

So they can be sure of understanding the material, SIXES like to move at their own pace, taking "breaks" when needed. By learning from role models whom they respect, they gradually become orientated to learning situations.

People outside a group or organization may be suspected of erroneous thinking. Out of fear of rejection, SIXES may suppress their individual thoughts to conform to group thinking.

Limitations occur when they experience creative thinking as threatening, especially when it appears to go against traditional thinking. Fears of exclusion from a group may inhibit SIXES from speaking their own minds. Self-doubts may keep them from coming across as convincing and clear. In their confusions and insecurity, they may give double or mixed messages.

SEVENS: POSITIVE THINKERS

The Positive thinking of SEVENS sees what can be more than what is, possibilities more than actualities. Their thinking explores different ways to enjoy life and work. They are apt to question whether a group is satisfied with the way things are going. Their minds are ever alert to new and exciting possibilities unfolding out of the future.

Because they live in a changing, multi-faceted world, SEVENS are curious about new ideas and innovative projects. Their thinking has a spreading quality whereby it branches unknowingly from one topic to another. Their minds experience connections between new and old topics, many of which are not so evident to more linear-thinking listeners. They offer fresh, creative insights into problems.

SEVENS like to discover new connections between things and combine ideas in creative outcomes. Events are planned to work out for their happiness. They like to keep moving toward worthwhile goals. However, unless their thinking is grounded in facts, it may be unrealistic and utopian.

The minds of SEVENS work constantly and quickly. Their thinking can shift rapidly from one idea to the next, providing a variety of options from which to choose. Large amounts of information can be scanned and integrated at a fast pace. Different viewpoints can be reframed in a positive perspective that makes them attractive.

They like myriad learning experiences that they can think about and process. Because a quick survey is enough to give them an idea of the content, they are ready to proceed quickly with new material. Their flexibility empowers them to adapt to a convergent approach that focuses on similarities or to a divergent strategy that attends to the differences in a situation.

Impatient with the status quo, SEVENS may want newness and change when the situation calls for stability. Troublesome details are apt to be overlooked. Impatient to get results, their thinking may not follow through in completing a project.

EIGHTS: DIALECTICAL THINKERS

The Dialectical thinking of EIGHTS fearlessly opposes the opinions of other people and assertively states their own views. Right at home with a conflict of viewpoints, they are good at keeping people from agreeing unnecessarily or indulging in uncreative "group-think." Disagreement is kept alive until it is sufficiently resolved.

They sense the differences and polarities that exist in the world. For every point, there is a counterpoint—Democrat and Republican, good and evil, negative and positive electric charges. When someone makes a point, EIGHTS counter with an opposite point.

Knowledge is power for EIGHTS. They may rely more on the forcefulness and power of their personalities than on the strength of their reasoning and evidence.

Once they get enough information they formulate a big picture in which parts are related to the whole. They like ideas to be defined with clarity so they can focus on their goals. Theories are put into practice to be tested. Quick briefings are preferred so they can get to the "heart" or substance of the material.

Challenging issues energize their thinking. Polite facades are penetrated to deal with "gut" issues. They are just as excited about how (process) they learn as they are about what (content) they think. Counterpoints are made by EIGHTS to positions stated by others in dialogue.

Underlying assumptions are questioned by EIGHTS. Gut feelings play an important role in making decisions. They direct actions to their goals for effective decisions. Complex situations are simplified as EIGHTS confront issues head on and debate the merits of solutions.

The EIGHTS' oppositional thinking may impede coming to agreement. Trivial issues that can be readily resolved may be needlessly debated. Their argumentative tendencies may unduly prolong discussion. Uncomfortable in static situations, they may lack patience to reflect before taking action. Once a problem is resolved and people agree, EIGHTS may lose interest and feel unchallenged.

NINES: HOLISTIC THINKERS

The Holistic thinking of NINES is integrative and unifies different ideas into a harmonious whole. Once they get an idea of the big picture, they can see how divergent viewpoints fit consistently together. They can find a common thread that ties disparate ideas into a harmonious whole. Motivated to get along with others, their thinking plays down the differences among people and balances opposing views.

Their thinking is also assimilative in the sense that new data is incorporated into a coherent whole. Their minds are able to grasp the inner patterns of unity and coherence within groups and organizations. The values and inputs of different individuals are smoothly incorporated into agreed on goals and concepts. Time is taken with the fine points of reasoning to be sure that conclusions are accurate. Their focus is on similarities amid differences to promote agreement and concord. They focus on the common ground that bridges people's different ideas. Similar things are classified together.

Holistic thinkers are apt to recognize connections and interdependencies that are not evident to other people. They sense the interconnectedness of the universe. All creatures are valued. Human beings are accepted as worthy of honor and as members of a fellowship with similar needs. They seek compromise and consensus, believing that truth is more apt to be present when people agree.

Once at ease with others, they feel comfortable in learning situations. They experience a gut awareness about feeling at home in their environment. Respect for authority enables them to be receptive to what they are told. They are open to a variety of input that empowers them to better understand before making a decision.

NINES may delay too long in making a decision in order to please everyone by listening to all divergent alternatives. They may agree to go whatever way the wind is blowing to avoid conflict. Going around a problem may appear better than confronting it.

Because dissimilarities tend to be suppressed, NINES may find it difficult to identify specific differences within the big picture. As a result, it may be hard for their attention to shift from the Gestalt foreground to the background and back. Unaware of variations, they have to make special efforts to identify priorities.

You are invited to respond to the following statements.

What are two strengths of your style of thinking?

How could you become more skillful in using the strengths you identified?
For example, if you are a THREE (Achiever and Practical Thinker) who listed
"communication," you may want to take a course in communication techniques.

Describe two ways you could apply your thinking strengths to your work or life.
For example, if you're an accurate and organized ONE (Perfecter and Idealist
Thinker), you could do the budgeting of finances in your relational or family life.

Describe a particular situation in which you have used your style of thinking effectively.

Have you inappropriately used or overused your thinking style? Please give an example.

Have the limits of your thinking style led to problems in your life and/or career? If so, describe how the problems arose from the limits of your thinking style.

What steps could you take to manage these problems effectively?

4

CHARTS OF THE
NINE THINKING STYLES

Each Enneagram type has characteristic ways of thinking and responding to various situations. The charts that follow will help to focus your understanding in several ways:

- When you are interacting with someone whose Enneagram type you do not know, the descriptions of typical behavior will help you to identify that person's type.

- You can use the information about the likes and dislikes of a particular Enneagram type to tailor your communication style to be most constructive.

- In problem-solving situations, use the information about how a person of a certain type reacts under stress. These cues can help you to avoid escalating a situation beyond the point of being productive.

Instructions: For each of the nine charts, think of a person you know who fits that type. Circle the descriptive phrases in the chart that seem to you most typical of that person. Then summarize for yourself the strengths and limitations of the thinking style of a person with that Enneagram type, as well as any reminder notes for yourself. You may want to refer to the information in Chapter 3 to help focus your thoughts.

THE IDEALIST THINKING OF ONES	
	Behavioral Hints
Apt to Appear:	Serious; relaxed when in agreement; uneasy with different viewpoints
Apt to Speak:	Directly, using a sermonizing or instructional approach with well-formulated statements; critically when disagreeing
Apt to Express:	Set ideas; stable views; conventional opinions
Tone:	Unemotional; well-modulated; disciplined; deliberate
Likes:	Short, direct, factual discussion of relevant matters
Apt to Ask:	"What is the correct procedure?" or "Does this agree with generally accepted principles or guidelines?"
Improves by:	Thinking positively; becoming optimistic about the future; looking for creative possibilities
Dislikes:	Small talk; unnecessary humor; disorganized thoughts
Under Stress:	May become oversensitive, self-distrusting, judgmental, critical; may resort to perfectionist thinking
Summary of Strengths:	
Summary of Limits:	
Notes:	

THE AFFECTIVE THINKING OF TWOS	
	Behavioral Hints
Apt to Appear:	Attentive; receptive; open; smiling; responsive
Apt to Speak:	Cordially; with one-on-one conversation; with care, advice, or flattery
Apt to Express:	Support; caring; sympathy
Tone:	Warm; friendly; concerned with personal values and feelings; focused on what is significant to people
Likes:	Listening to others' feelings; tactfulness; appreciation
Apt to Ask:	"How does this help people?" or "How will people feel about this?"
Improves by:	Becoming aware of own genuine needs; individualistic thinking
Dislikes:	Impersonal responses; treating people as data or statistics; lack of appreciation
Under Stress:	May feel hurt; may manipulate by flattery; may become angry; may use dictatorial thinking
Summary of Strengths:	
Summary of Limits:	
Notes:	

THE PRACTICAL THINKING OF THREES	
	Behavioral Hints
Apt to Appear:	Sociable; busy; self-assured; polished
Apt to Speak:	Persuasively; quickly; with popular opinions, illustrations, or examples
Apt to Express:	Simple ideas; interesting stories
Tone:	Enthusiastic; energetic; may appear insincere
Likes:	Down-to-earth ideas; results; quick solutions; progress reports; winning images
Apt to Ask:	"What's the goal?" or "How will we get results?"
Improves by:	Relating well to others; being open to the broader interests of others; thinking of the good of the group
Dislikes:	Too much theory or analysis; inefficient thinking; slow or dull conversation
Under Stress:	May become bored or apathetic; may take on workaholic tendencies; may use passive or accommodative thinking
Summary of Strengths:	
Summary of Limits:	
Notes:	

THE INDIVIDUALIST THINKING OF FOURS	
	Behavioral Hints
Apt to Appear:	Expressive; different; honest; genuine
Apt to Speak:	With emotion and sensitivity
Apt to Express:	Feelings; original points of view; values
Tone:	Reflecting moods: happy or sad; serious or funny
Likes:	Feeling-level conversation about people and problems
Apt to Ask:	"How do people feel about it?" or "Will it really be good for them?"
Improves by:	Becoming more aware of own worth; maintaining stable thinking, with standards and goals
Dislikes:	Insensitivity; impersonal systems; disrespect; discussions dominated by facts
Under Stress:	May be easily hurt; may manipulate; may use self-absorbed, emotional thinking
Summary of Strengths:	
Summary of Limits:	
Notes:	

THE ANALYTICAL THINKING OF FIVES	
	Behavioral Hints
Apt to Appear:	Detached; inquisitive; observant; knowledgeable; hard to know
Apt to Speak:	Calmly; abstractly; by summarizing essential information; with qualified statements
Apt to Express:	Ideas systematically and clearly using supportive data; general, abstract principles
Tone:	Unemotional; disciplined; deliberate; inquiring
Likes:	Observing situations; logical analysis of problems; speculative or philosophical discussions
Apt to Ask:	"What is the evidence for the claim?" or "Is that conclusion logical?"
Improves by:	Becoming aware of feelings; using action-oriented thinking
Dislikes:	Pointless or superficial conversation; unclear ideas; emotional overstatements
Under Stress:	May withdraw; may lack follow through; may use impulsive or self-seeking thinking
Summary of Strengths:	
Summary of Limits:	
Notes:	

THE AUTHORITATIVE THINKING OF SIXES	
	Behavioral Hints
Apt to Appear:	Cooperative and attentive, especially in trustworthy groups; smiling
Apt to Speak:	Warmly within own group, carefully in other conversations; maintaining established opinions
Apt to Express:	Traditional ideas; concepts about rules, obligations, customs
Tone:	Trusting and believing within own group; doubtful or tentative with outsiders
Likes:	Reliable thinking; loyalty to group standards; discussions about the group
Apt to Ask:	"What are our responsibilities?" or "Who can we count on?"
Improves by:	Self-reliant thinking; focus on inner resources; stable self-worth
Dislikes:	Belittling traditions; individualistic thinking; criticisms of culture or customs; ambiguity
Under Stress:	May lack inner authority; may vacillate; may use indecisive, opportunistic thinking
Summary of Strengths:	
Summary of Limits:	
Notes:	

THE POSITIVE THINKING OF SEVENS	
	Behavioral Hints
Apt to Appear:	Responsive; enthusiastic; direct; spontaneous; smiling
Apt to Speak:	Excitedly; with stories and lively metaphors
Apt to Express:	Humor; verbal feedback
Tone:	Positive; agreeable; may be glib
Likes:	Quick, brief discussion of new strategies and projects; brainstorming
Apt to Ask:	"What is on the planning agenda?" or "What are the positive payoffs?"
Improves by:	Focusing on priorities; deeper reflections on values in life and work
Dislikes:	Excessive talk about theories; pessimism; routine; critical supervisors; humorless conversation
Under Stress:	May think impulsively; may become agitated, nervous, and immoderate in speech; may become rigid and intolerant of others' ideas
Summary of Strengths:	
Summary of Limits:	
Notes:	

THE DIALECTICAL THINKING OF EIGHTS	
	Behavioral Hints
Apt to Appear:	Challenging; skeptical; confrontive; controlling
Apt to Speak:	Bluntly and forcefully; directly and confidently
Apt to Express:	Opposite viewpoints and commands; agreement and disagreement promptly
Tone:	Questioning; argumentative or dominating
Likes:	Debate; assertiveness in discussions; strong viewpoints
Apt to Ask:	"Who is in charge?" or "How much authority do I have?"
Improves by:	Using leadership qualities to empower others to think for themselves; using caring thinking
Dislikes:	Domineering thinkers; restrictions on ideas; simplistic views
Under Stress:	May react rather than act; may use overbearing, aggressive thinking
Summary of Strengths:	
Summary of Limits:	
Notes:	

THE HOLISTIC THINKING OF NINES	
	Behavioral Hints
Apt to Appear:	Attentive; receptive; nodding and smiling
Apt to Speak:	Agreeably; calmly; in a matter-of-fact manner
Apt to Express:	Acceptable or generally standard ideas; noncontroversial topics
Tone:	Even; monotone
Likes:	Calm, factual discussion; agreement
Apt to Ask:	"How can things run smoothly?" or "How can we resolve the disagreement?"
Improves by:	Active thinking; action-oriented ideas
Dislikes:	Conflicting ideas; tense discussion; changing viewpoints
Under Stress:	May deny problems; may use passive, indecisive thinking
Summary of Strengths:	
Summary of Limits:	
Notes:	

5

FOCUS OF THINKING

One of the most important elements of thinking is focus. Focus is the direction that your thinking takes. Direction gives purpose, goals, and clear expectations to a person's thinking. However, different personalities focus on different aspects of a goal and commit themselves by using their talents and thinking to realize the goal.

Each thinking style focuses on a particular facet of reality as indicated in Figure 3. When you experience congruence between your thinking style and the situations around you, you are apt to feel comfortable and at home. You realize that people have a need for your way of thinking as well as appreciating how others think. Therefore, because you feel a part of that group or organization, you find fulfillment in meeting goals.

Thinking Style	Focus
ONES: Idealist thinking	Correct order; quality performance or work
TWOS: Affective thinking	Human needs; service
THREES: Practical thinking	Results/outcomes; competition
FOURS: Individualist thinking	Uniqueness of each person; distinctive expression
FIVES: Analytical thinking	Rational structure; critical thinking
SIXES: Authoritative thinking	Human relationships; commitment
SEVENS: Positive thinking	Satisfaction; innovation
EIGHTS: Dialectical thinking	Power/authority; action
NINES: Holistic thinking	Agreement and harmony; routine activities

Figure 3. Focus of Thinking

ONES

Order and Quality.   Important elements in life and work are order among people and tasks, and the performance of the operations according to correct procedures. ONES focus their attention on the correct ordering of tasks, the quality of work, and fairness among people.

TWOS

Needs and Service.   TWOS tend to focus on the needs of people, showing empathy for the needs and concerns of others. They exercise authority in the service of others. TWOS like the approval and gratitude they receive from helping others in need.

THREES

Results and Competition.   THREES focus on the mission and results of tasks. They desire to experience success and compete to produce outcomes and make favorable impressions.

FOURS

Person and Distinctiveness.   FOURS focus on individuals and are very much aware of how important it is to preserve a distinct identity in a relationship or organization. For that reason, FOURS want the climate of a situation to be humanistic so that each person is respected for his or her personal worth and dignity.

FIVES

Structure and Rationality.   FIVES focus on the rational structure and intelligible systems in the world to be sure they make sense. Every part of their world needs to fit consistently within the whole and work systematically for the whole. FIVES follow the economic law of "Don't multiply parts without necessity." It is not surprising that they want to save time, money, and energy.

THE ENNEAGRAM PERSONALITY PORTRAITS

SIXES

Relationship and Commitment.   An important feature in life and work for SIXES is how well people relate. They focus their attention on promoting trust, cooperation, and commitment to one another and to groups. They like the decisions of authority to be clear so others will know their duties. Order and stability in interpersonal relationships is important to them.

SEVENS

Satisfaction and Innovation.   SEVENS focus on the satisfaction of people. They are very much aware of how important it is for individuals to be happy at what they are doing. SEVENS like to see situations as alive and developing, open to innovative ideas and projects.

EIGHTS

Power and Action.   EIGHTS focus on power, which is why they like being in positions of authority. There they can effectively mobilize people to take action and accomplish tasks in the way the EIGHTS want them to be done.

NINES

Harmony and Routine.   NINES focus on harmonious operations and the stability that comes with routine. They want to see people getting along together and collaborating for peace.

You are invited to answer the following questions:

What is the focus of your thinking style?

How does your personality fit the focus of your thinking style?

What uses do you make of your thinking style at home and/or at work?

6

TRANSFORMATION OF
THINKING STYLE

To this point, we have examined the characteristics of the various Enneagram types. In this chapter, the focus is on how the types interrelate. You will note the Enneagram diagram (Figure 4) includes arrows: One points toward each type and one leads away from each type. These can be referred to as the "arrows of development." Another feature of the Enneagram diagram is the arrangement of the types. Each type has two adjacent types, which represent the "wings of development." The sections that follow describe how to use the information about arrows of development and wings of development to enhance your thinking style.

ARROWS OF DEVELOPMENT

Stretching your mind beyond its comfort zone can develop your thinking skills. The arrows on the Enneagram diagram refer to the directions of development and decline for each thinking style. Therefore, starting with your dominant thinking style, you can choose to journey on the path to development or on the path to decline.

See the Enneagram diagram that follows. The direction of development involves traveling against the arrow that points toward your style—think of it as swimming against the current in order to grow. For example, the way of development for the FIVE is to move *against* its arrow, toward the EIGHT. On the other hand, the direction of decline consists of journeying with the arrow that points away from a particular type. Using the example again of a FIVE, the path of decline would be to go *with* the arrow, toward the SEVEN.

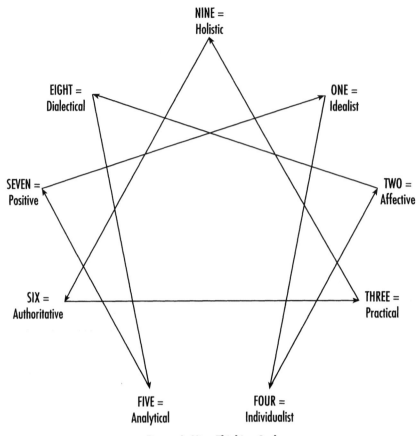

Figure 4. Nine Thinking Styles

Therefore, each style can be mind-draining or mind-serving, depending on where it falls on what is called the line of development and decline, as shown in Figure 5:

Mind-Draining Decline  Mind-Serving Development

Figure 5. The Line of Development and Decline

On this line, a person's thinking may be gradually progressing toward being more mind-serving or regressing toward being more mind-draining. For example, TWOS become more mind-serving as they advance along the way of development toward the Individualist thinking of the FOUR, growing in awareness of their own individual needs as well as others' needs. TWOS become more mind-draining when they regress along the way of decline toward the EIGHT and fall into Dictatorial thinking.

In the table that follows (Figure 6), the nine Enneagram types are listed, along with the directions of development and decline for each.

Way of Decline, Toward Type _____	Dominant Enneagram Type	Way of Development, Toward Type_____
FOUR: Oversensitive Moody, self-doubting, self-pity	ONE	SEVEN: Positive Outlook Optimistic, joyful, spontaneous
EIGHT: Domineering Arrogant, vindictive, oppositional	TWO	FOUR: Aware of Own Needs Sensitive, creative, compassionate
NINE: Inactive Unresponsive, indolent, passive	THREE	SIX: Larger Interest Trusting, loyal, cooperative
TWO: Egocentric Possessive, jealous, manipulative	FOUR	ONE: Unique Goodness Objective, stable, self-disciplined
SEVEN: Impulsive Immoderate, unstable, indulgent	FIVE	EIGHT: Assertive Confident, stable, self-disciplined
THREE: Aggresive Self-inflated, opportunistic, deceptive	SIX	NINE: Secure Stable, peaceful, accepting
ONE: Obsessive Perfectionistic, opinionated, intolerant	SEVEN	FIVE: Depth Experience Insightful, focused, understanding
FIVE: Unfeeling Withdrawn, fearful, unrealistic	EIGHT	TWO: Altruistic Caring, helpful, friendly
SIX: Anxious Indecisive, insecure, overdependent	NINE	THREE: Active Motivated, energetic, productive

Figure 6. Directions of Development and Decline

WINGS OF DEVELOPMENT

Another direction of development is to stretch your "wings." According to the Enneagram, no individual is simply one type or thinking style alone. Each individual is characterized by his or her basic dominant type and an auxiliary style called "the wing." The wings are the types adjacent to a person's dominant type; for example, FIVE can have a FOUR-wing or a SIX-wing.

Both wings impact a particular type. This means that the Idealist thinking of the ONE can participate in the Affective thinking of the TWO or in the Holistic thinking of the NINE. Participation in the wings gives each individual his or her distinctive personality type and thinking style. In most people, one of the wings tends to predominate while the other functions at least potentially. Thus, for example, a Practical thinking THREE who is task-oriented can actuate the potentialities of the FOUR's Individualist thinking or the TWO's Affective thinking in order to become more people-oriented.

In the table that follows (Figure 7), the dominant Enneagram types are illustrated along with their balancing wings.

Balanced by Wing #	Personality Type	Enneagram Number	Thinking Style	Balanced by Wing #
NINE Peacefulness Relaxation Easygoing approach	ONE Anger Perfection Seriousness	ONE	ONE Concern for tasks Correction Fairness	TWO Concern for people Caring Compassion
ONE Saying "no" Thinking of self Task priority	TWO Saying "yes" Caring for others People priority	TWO	TWO Relating one-on-one Cooperation Satisfactory relationships	THREE Gregariousness Competition Successful projects
TWO Concern for others Collaboration Friendliness	THREE Success-mindedness Competition Efficiency	THREE	THREE Image-consciousness Superficiality Success at work	FOUR Genuine responsiveness Depth of feelings Creative expression
THREE Action Group-orientation Efficiency	FOUR Feelings Individual focus Sensitivity	FOUR	FOUR Feelings Sensitivity Changing emotions	FIVE Thinking Logic Detachment
FOUR Connected with personal feelings Sensitivity Intuition	FIVE Detached from personal feelings Objectivity Reasoning	FIVE	FIVE Noninvolvement Individuality Detachment	SIX Dutifulness Group identification Commitment
FIVE Inner wisdom Broad world view Individual thinking	SIX Insecurity about self Group-orientation Authority focus	SIX	SIX Fear of change Security of rules Dutifulness	SEVEN Excitement of innovation Spontaneity Playfulness
SIX Moderation Present duty Persistence	SEVEN "More is better" Enjoyment Avoiding unpleasantness	SEVEN	SEVEN Optimism Childlike tendencies Leisure	EIGHT Pessimism Strength Intensity
SEVEN Responsiveness Planning Joy	EIGHT Assertiveness Mobilization Justice	EIGHT	EIGHT Decisiveness Intensity Forcefulness	NINE Calmness Relaxation Receptivity
EIGHT Assertiveness Energy Facing disagreement	NINE Accommodation Easygoing nature Getting agreement	NINE	NINE Peacemaking Self-possession Receptivity	ONE Fairness Task-orientation Reforming

Figure 7. Wings of Development

Against the background of the arrows and wings and your knowledge of thinking styles, you are invited to answer the following questions:

What new thinking style do you develop as you travel along the arrow of development from your dominant thinking style?

List five strategies of the new thinking style:

a.

b.

c.

d.

e.

What activities enable you to practice those strategies?

Five Ways to Improve Each of the Nine Thinking Styles

Instructions: Locate your type and style number. Put checkmarks in the boxes that might help your thinking style.

ONES

- ❏ Keep a positive attitude by looking on the bright side of challenging issues.

- ❏ Listen to people who talk about the value of high standards and superordinate goals.

- ❏ Break through rigid conceptual frameworks by brainstorming for new, alternative suggestions without instinctively rejecting others' ideas because of their shortcomings.

- ❏ Balance the right procedure and "shoulds" of standards with genuine concerns for persons and flexible, creative application of principles.

- ❏ Stop and listen to others' ideas and suggestions to find their relevance, even though at first glance they seem to have no relation to the subject at hand.

TWOS

- ❏ Shift perspective from an outer to an inner insight that empowers you to discover unique talents and abilities.

- ❏ Take time to discover your own real personal and professional needs that require self-support and self-development.

- ❏ Believe in your own genuine value as a person and the quality of your supportive thinking as a way to evoke gratitude from others.

- ❏ Balance your helpful nature with a disciplined focus on quality performance based on clear operating standards and with a take-action attitude to complete tasks efficiently.

- ❏ Affirm your self-image with positive self-talk such as, "I am caring and helpful" or "I am supportive and giving."

THREES

- ❏ Expand professional vision beyond personal career advancement to include a larger organization context that adds broader meaning to your enterprising efforts.

- ❏ Develop the supportive side of your nature by acknowledging, complimenting, and promoting the special thinking talents of individual people.

- ❏ Try to anticipate the long-term consequences of your decisions, asking yourself what will happen five years from now if something occurs.

- ❏ Motivate others to be more cooperative than competitive, for friends work better together on a team than opponents.

- ❏ Balance your passion for achievement with a sensitivity that respects the limits of others.

FOURS

- ❏ Stabilize your personal thinking style by functioning more from your reality-oriented head (which objectively confronts tasks) rather from your feeling-oriented heart, (which can vacillate and confuse).

- ❏ Follow clear standards and principles so decisions can be made with deliberation rather than impulsiveness.

- ❏ Balance empathy for people's personal feelings with disciplined thinking about the pros and cons for getting a job done.

- ❏ Set specific results you want to attain and spell out clearly each step that is useful to obtain desired outcomes.

- ❏ Overcome the tendency to withdraw in the face of hard realities to a world of fantasy by taking action to accomplish tasks.

FIVES

- ❏ Balance rational analysis of problems with a sensitive perception of people's feelings and the impact of issues on individual people.

- Learn to be open to reports of feelings as well as intelligence as sources of information about projects and persons.

- Risk putting ideas into action and sharing your vision with others who can benefit from a wealth of insights.

- Learn to assert yourself with enthusiasm and develop confidence in your actions to get effective responses from people.

- Develop team thinking by inviting an exchange of ideas among persons and a collaborative approach to solving problems.

SIXES

- Acknowledge whatever real fears and apprehensions you may have about your thinking abilities, remembering that fears are intended to be servants to inform thinking and energize actions, not rulers to control them.

- Remember: If you fear something could go wrong in the organization, you may be right, and that is worth knowing.

- Break through negative, anxious thinking to positive, exciting ideas about all the possibly good outcomes that could overwhelm you.

- Develop inner strength with positive self-affirmations such as, "I am sure of my abilities" or "I am confident of my views," or "I trust in my decisions."

- Steer your thinking style on a clear, assertive course between the Scylla of obsequiousness and the Charybdis of hostility.

SEVENS

- Look beyond instant payoffs to discover what is good for the people or an organization in the long run.

- Moderate enthusiasm for many projects by focusing energies on completing a few tasks at a time.

- Deepen appreciation of your work and life by taking time now and then to ask yourself, "What's happening here?" and "What function am I performing?"

- Motivate people with enthusiasm to become a team by finding satisfaction in cooperating with each other on tasks.

❑ Balance creative brainstorming and innovation with practical, realistic steps for completing each project.

EIGHTS

❑ Balance caring for power with the power of caring, helping, and inspiring others so thinking can be an a tool of service rather than of domination.

❑ Play the devil's advocate by asking, "What will go wrong?" if a solution is implemented.

❑ Use your natural gift of leadership reasonably and responsibly to accomplish great enterprises and gain the heartfelt respect of workers.

❑ Harmonize your independent thinking and self-determination with reliance on the talents and abilities of others.

❑ Learn the value of harmony by mediating opposing views and reaching consensus conclusions rather than imposing solutions on problems.

NINES

❑ Practice harmonizing opposing ideas within a common framework.

❑ Sacrifice a passing peace to face the hard reality of conflicts and work them through to a lasting peace.

❑ Learn to be assertive in stating your own views and plans without over-accommodating others' interests.

❑ Learn to be proactive in setting clear goals and following up with action to get results.

❑ Prioritize desired outcomes to facilitate decisions and manage changes in a smooth way.

7

NINE APPROACHES TO PROBLEM SOLVING

Results can be creatively produced by problem-solving. Identifying your individual style of problem-solving empowers you to use your talents creatively. Therefore, knowing this information about your work team allows each member to contribute to the overall effectiveness of the team in his or her own way.

Each Enneagram type tends to focus on a particular aspect of problem solving, as follows:

1. ONES, SIXES, and NINES focus on facts.
2. FOURS and SEVENS consider possibilities.
3. FIVES concentrate on meanings.
4. ONES and FIVES attend to methods.
5. TWOS, FOURS, and NINES attend to people.
6. THREES and EIGHTS center on results.

As illustrated in the diagram that follows (Figure 8), progress in problem solving requires following the steps sequentially.

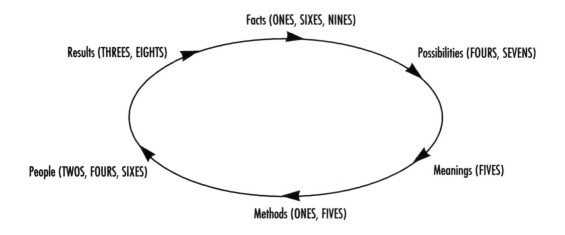

Facts (ONES, SIXES, NINES)

Results (THREES, EIGHTS)

Possibilities (FOURS, SEVENS)

People (TWOS, FOURS, SIXES)

Meanings (FIVES)

Methods (ONES, FIVES)

Figure 8. Model of Problem Solving

PROBLEM-SOLVING STEPS

Clarify and define the problem with information, facts (ONES, SIXES, NINES) or data. Make realistic observations and descriptions of the situation as it exists. Identify what is unknown, distinguish relevant from irrelevant information, and visualize the problem. Draw diagrams and organize data tables.

Brainstorm (FOURS and SEVENS) for all possible solutions. Use your imagination to picture all possible alternative courses of action. Get the big picture, using analogies and metaphors to map out the possibilities. At this stage, withhold judgments about the usefulness or validity of a course of action. Write down the alternatives so you can think about them and refer back to them when necessary.

Understand how each solution throws light on the problem, reflecting on the significance and consequences (FIVES) of each. Ask the right questions about the meaning and implications of each course of action. Use theories or models to help you understand each course of action, weighing each one's benefits and disadvantages. How do the short-term effects compare with long-range effects? Identify and list the successive steps of each course of action to be sure that each step leads toward the desired result. Rank each course of action according to its effectiveness in achieving the preferred outcome.

Assess the process and results (ONES and FIVES).   If difficulties arise, reexamine the method in light of new data, a better understanding of the situation, unforeseen events, or changes in goals or circumstances. It is important to use the correct method and to evaluate the validity of the results. Are you sure you have solved the problem? How can you be sure? Check the results.

Deliberate about the alternatives in terms of their impacts on people, including yourself (TWOS, FOURS, NINES).   How will people be affected by the course of action that is most effective in achieving the desired result? How do you feel about these effects on people? How do you feel about the advantages and drawbacks? What values are important to you?

Decide what course of action to pursue (THREES, EIGHTS) to get your preferred result. Then do it.

Read the particular functions of your type and others' types in the diagram that follows (Figure 9):

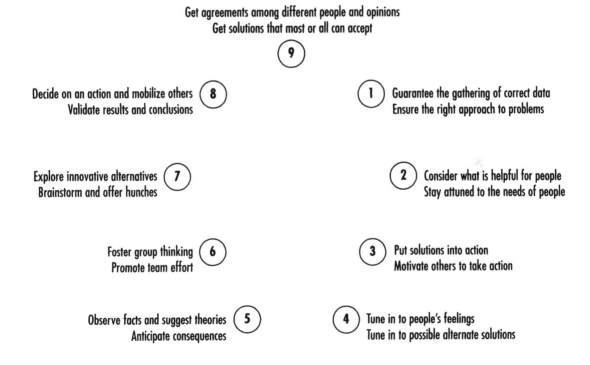

Get agreements among different people and opinions
Get solutions that most or all can accept

9

Decide on an action and mobilize others **8**
Validate results and conclusions

1 Guarantee the gathering of correct data
Ensure the right approach to problems

Explore innovative alternatives **7**
Brainstorm and offer hunches

2 Consider what is helpful for people
Stay attuned to the needs of people

Foster group thinking **6**
Promote team effort

3 Put solutions into action
Motivate others to take action

Observe facts and suggest theories **5**
Anticipate consequences

4 Tune in to people's feelings
Tune in to possible alternate solutions

Figure 9. Personal Creative Problem Solving

Then answer the following questions:

What are your talents or strengths as a team in problem solving?

What are your blind spots or limitations as a team? In other words, are you lacking some style(s) of problem solving? What are they?

Collaboration among team members with different talents is an effective approach to problem solving. There is no one way to solve problems that applies equally well to all situations. Some situations require critical thinking and standard procedures. Other problems may require affective thinking that operates more from the heart than from the head. The needs of the situation dictate the specific problem-solving response and the type or types most likely to lead each step (Figure 10).

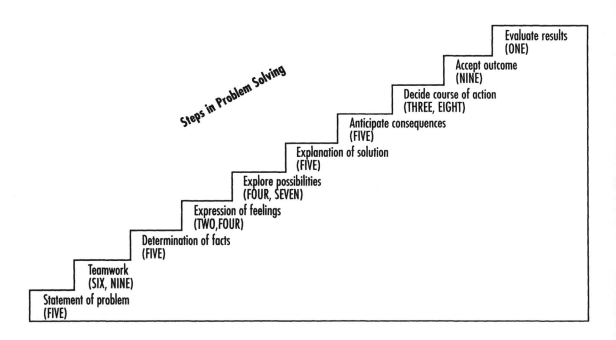

Figure 10. Steps in Problem Solving

After you are clear about the contribution of your professional style to problem solving, your team is invited to choose a problem that needs a solution. When you or another group member addresses the problem, observe how as well as what each person says. Use the log that follows (Figure 11) to keep track of the responses, writing specific examples that illustrate the particular types and functions in problem solving.

Types	Functions	Observations
ONES	Assure correct understanding of facts. Identify the exact situation. Assess procedures and results.	
TWOS	Focus on the impact on people. Identify what is helpful for people.	
THREES	Get results. Motivate people. Take action.	
FOURS	Explore people's feeling about alternative solutions. Examine the personal significance of each alternative.	
FIVES	Observe data. Analyze ways of understanding the situation. Examine the consequences of each alternative.	
SIXES	Make it a team effort. Learn what the majority thinks.	
SEVENS	Explore new ideas or brainstorm different ways of doing the job. Seek ways to change the situation.	
EIGHTS	Decide what to do. Rally people. Take action.	
NINES	Work for agreement or consensus on data. Look for opposing opinions and views.	

Figure 11. Log of Problem-Solving Responses

With the information gathered from your observations, answer the following questions:

What contribution do you make to the process of problem solving?

How can you improve your effectiveness in problem solving?

8

TAKING ACTION

Knowledge, to be useful, needs to be put into action. You have participated individually and with others in the experience of thinking about thinking. This last activity is to help you complete the journey with "a bang and not a whimper" (T.S. Eliot).

The fully functioning human being actualizes peak self-empowerment by consistently applying insights and skills to his or her life. You are invited to complete the following statements:

1. I learned that my thinking is ...

2. I realize that my thinking has talents or strengths such as …

3. I know that I can develop my thinking by …

4. I have decided to put the following ideas into action:

   a.

   b.

   c,

5. I will take action on these things by doing these specific behaviors:

   a.

   b.

   c.

6. I will check my progress at least once a week by observing, reflecting, and completing the following statements:

    a. I see a difference in myself when I …

    b. I grasp a difference in my thinking when I …

You are invited to share your responses with others. Remember: Actions speak louder than words.

9

SELECTED BIBLIOGRAPHY

Aspell, D.D., & Aspell, P.J. (1990). *Chart of the Enneagram Personality Types.* San Antonio, TX: Lifewings® Ltd.

Aspell, D.D., & Aspell, P.J. (1991). *Profiles of the Enneagram: Ways of Coming Home to Yourself.* San Antonio, TX: Lifewings® Ltd.

Aspell, D.D., & Aspell, P.J. (1992). *Unlimited Empowerment: Discovering and Enhancing Your Personal Professional Life via the Enneagram.* San Antonio, TX: Lifewings® Ltd.

Aspell, D.D., & Aspell, P.J. (1993). *Empowering Relationships: Discovering and Enhancing Your Personal and Interpersonal Life via the Enneagram.* San Antonio, TX: Lifewings® Ltd.

Aspell, D.D., & Aspell, P.J. (1994). *Building Better Relationships with People.* San Antonio, TX: Lifewings® Ltd.

Aspell, D.D., & Aspell, P.J. (1994). *Career and Life Management.* San Antonio, TX: Lifewings® Ltd.

Aspell, D.D., & Aspell, P.J. (1994). *Chart of the Nine Enneagram Personality Types and Professional Styles.* San Antonio, TX: Lifewings® Ltd.

Aspell, D.D., & Aspell, P.J. (1994). *Creating Teams and Building Teamwork.* San Antonio, TX: Lifewings® Ltd.

Aspell, D.D., & Aspell, P.J. (1994). *The Discovery and Development of Effective Personal Leadership.* San Antonio, TX: Lifewings® Ltd.

Aspell, D.D., & Aspell, P.J. (1994). *Profiles of the Nine Personal Professional Enneagram Styles.* San Antonio, TX: Lifewings® Ltd.

Aspell, D.D., & Aspell, P.J. (1995). *Discovering Yourself and Developing Your Style of Leadership, Supervision, and Counseling.* San Antonio, TX: Lifewings® Ltd.

Aspell, D.D., & Aspell, P.J. (1995). *Enneagram Communication Styles.* San Antonio, TX: Lifewings® Ltd.

Aspell, D.D., & Aspell, P.J. (1995). *Enneagram Learning Styles.* San Antonio, TX: Lifewings® Ltd.

Aspell, D.D., & Aspell, P.J. (1995). *Enneagram Teaching and Training Styles.* San Antonio, TX: Lifewings® Ltd.

Aspell, D.D., & Aspell, P.J. (1995). *Enneagram Thinking and Problem Solving Styles.* San Antonio, TX: Lifewings® Ltd.

Aspell, D.D., & Aspell, P.J. (1995). *Enneagram Transparencies.* San Antonio, TX: Lifewings® Ltd.

Aspell, D.D., & Aspell, P.J. (1995). *How to Use the Enneagram for Effective Counseling.* San Antonio, TX: Lifewings® Ltd.

Aspell, D.D., & Aspell, P.J. (1995). Leadership Styles and the Enneagram, in J.W. Pfeiffer (Ed.), *The 1995 Annual: Volume 1, Training* (pp. 227-241). San Francisco: Pfeiffer, An Imprint of Jossey-Bass Inc., Publishers.

Aspell, D.D., & Aspell, P.J. (1995). *Letting Go of Irritants.* San Antonio, TX: Lifewings® Ltd.

Aspell, D.D., & Aspell, P.J. (1995). *Managing Conflict the Enneagram Way.* San Antonio, TX: Lifewings® Ltd.

Aspell, D.D., & Aspell, P.J. (1995). *Using the Enneagram to Empower Organizations.* San Antonio, TX: Lifewings® Ltd.

Aspell, D.D., & Aspell, P.J. (1995). *Using the Enneagram to Build Better Marital Relationships.* San Antonio, TX: Lifewings® Ltd.

Aspell, D.D., & Aspell, P.J. (1996). *The Eloquent Enneagrammer: Quality Presentation and Speaking.* San Antonio, TX: Lifewings® Ltd.

Aspell, D.D., & Aspell, P.J. (1996). *The Enterprising Enneagrammer: How to Use the Enneagram to Generate Sales.* San Antonio, TX: Lifewings® Ltd.

Aspell, D.D., & Aspell, P.J. (1996). *Journey from Type to Archetype: Jungian Personality Type Inventory and Archetype Inventory* . San Antonio, TX: Lifewings® Ltd.

Aspell, D.D., & Aspell, P.J. (1996). *The Jungian Personality Type Inventory* . San Antonio, TX: Lifewings® Ltd.

Aspell, D.D., & Aspell, P.J. (1996). *The Lawyer's Enneagram.* San Antonio, TX: Lifewings® Ltd.

Aspell, D.D., & Aspell, P.J. (1996). *The Nine Enneagram Negotiation Styles.* San Antonio, TX: Lifewings® Ltd.

Aspell, D.D., & Aspell, P.J. (1996). *Portraits of Enneagram Relationships: Nine Relational and Forty-Five Interpersonal Enneagram Relationships.* San Antonio, TX: Lifewings® Ltd.

Covey, S.R. (1990). *The Seven Habits of Highly Effective People.* New York: Simon & Schuster.

Covey, S.R. (1991). *Principle-Centered Leadership.* New York: Simon & Schuster.

Forster, S., & O'Hanrahan, R. (1994). *Understanding Personality Types in the Workplace.* Oakland, CA: Authors.

Palmer, H. (1995). *The Enneagram in Love and Work.* San Francisco: HarperCollins.

Printed and bound by CPI Group (UK) Ltd, Croydon, CR0 4YY

10/06/2025

14686746-0001